CHRISTMAS
Follow~the~Dots

Suzanne Ross

DOVER PUBLICATIONS, INC.
Mineola, New York

Bibliographical Note

Christmas Follow-the-Dots is a new work, first published by Dover
Publications, Inc., in 2003.

International Standard Book Number: 0-486-42999-7

Manufactured in the United States of America
Dover Publications, Inc., 31 East 2nd Street, Mineola, N.Y. 11501

NOTE

This little book is full of Christmas fun! Each puzzle page contains a picture. You will connect the dots to complete the picture. First, read the hint below the puzzle. Then, using a pencil or a pen, start at dot number 1 and draw a line to dot number 2, and from dot number 2 to dot number 3, and so on. Some puzzles have letters, so start at dot A and go from A to B to C, and so on. There is a list of solutions at the back of the book in case you have trouble. When all of the dots are connected, have even more fun by coloring in the pictures. Are you ready? Now follow the dots and have some Christmas fun!

Santa's elves are tying something. Follow the
dots to find out what it is!

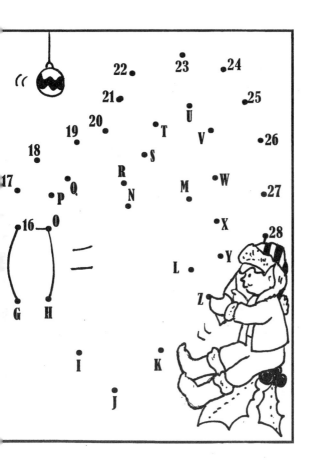

22 • 23 • • 24
21 • • 25
20 Ü
19 • • T V • • 26
18 • S •
17 • R • W
• P Q N • M • • 27
16 0 • X
G H • Y
L • 28
Z •
I K
j

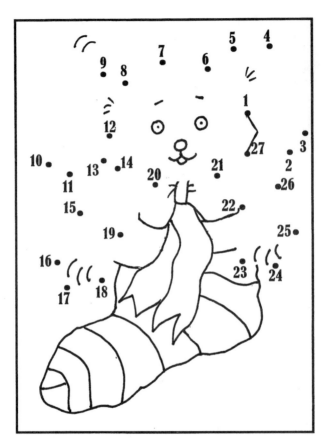

Here's something cute in a stocking. Follow the dots
to see it.

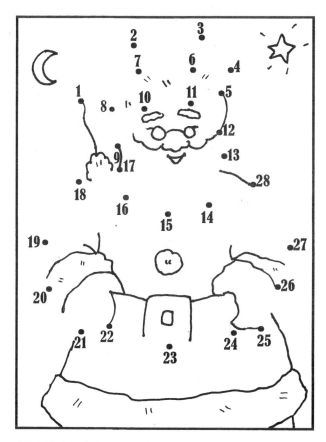

Ho! Ho! Ho! Connect the dots to see this jolly fellow.

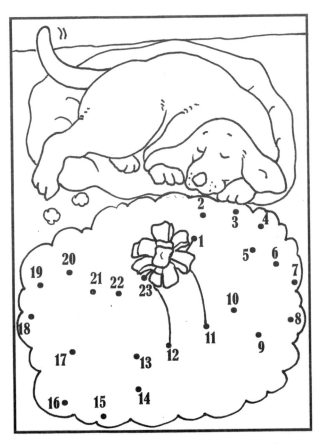

Barney is dreaming of something he wants for Christmas. What can it be?

What does Santa have? Follow the dots to find out.

Some people receive many of these at Christmas time.
What is it?

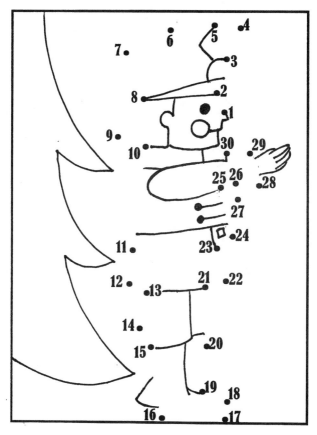

Here is a Christmas present from long ago. Follow
the dots to see a picture of it.

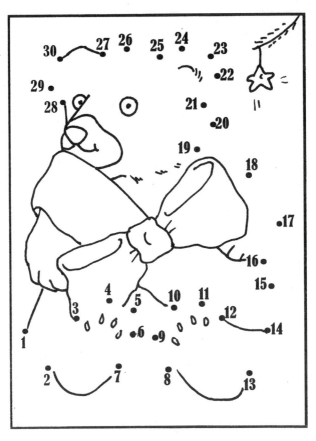

This cuddly gift will make a child very happy! Let's see what it is.

Here is something that you can hang on your door at Christmas.

This girl loves music. Follow the dots to see a picture
of what she is holding.

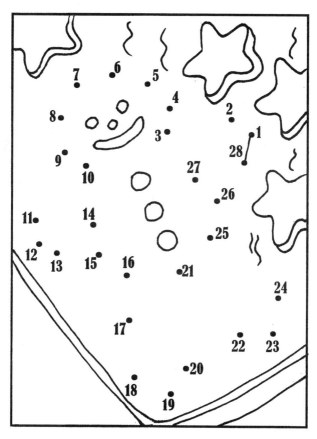

Here's a special cookie for the holiday. What do you think it might be?

This might be in front of a house during Christmas.
Connect the dots to see it.

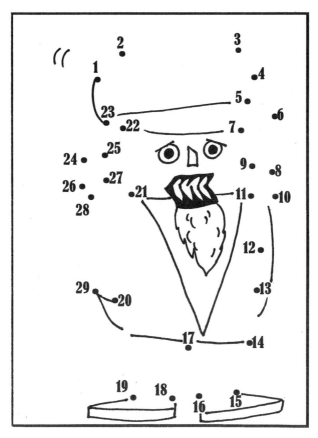

You might see this character in a popular Christmas ballet. What is it?

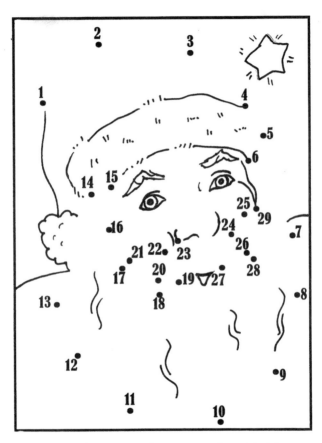

Follow the dots to see who everyone is waiting for at Christmas time.

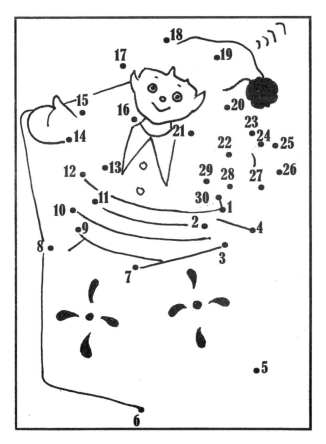

This toy makes noise when it pops open. Connect the
dots to see what it is.

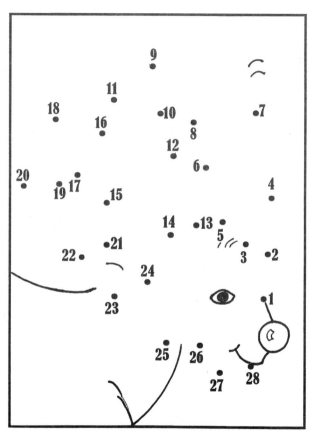

Follow the dots to see a picture of this famous
Christmas character.

This elf has something that Santa needs to wear.
What might it be?

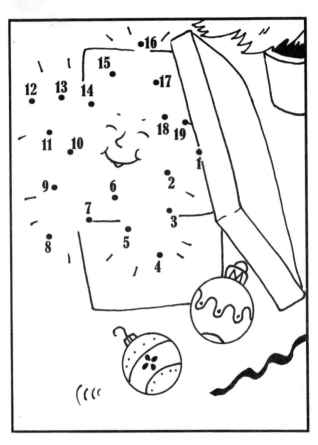

The decoration in this box will go on the Christmas tree. What is it?

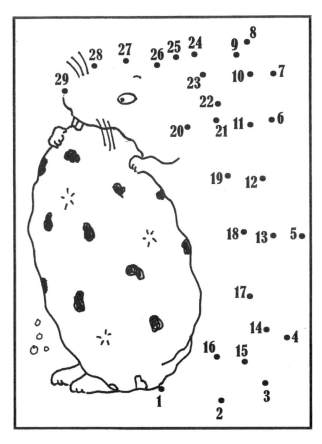

Who is nibbling on a cookie? Follow the dots
to find out!

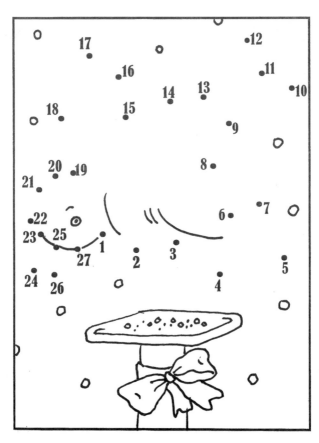

The children left out some seeds on Christmas
morning. Find out who ate them.

Follow the dots to see what is frozen to the roof
of this house.

Santa has a hard time reaching some children. See how he solves the problem!

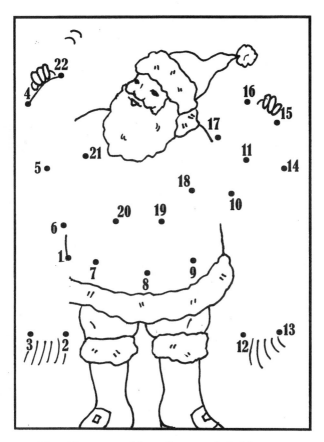

Mrs. Claus gave this to Santa to help him stay warm. What is it?

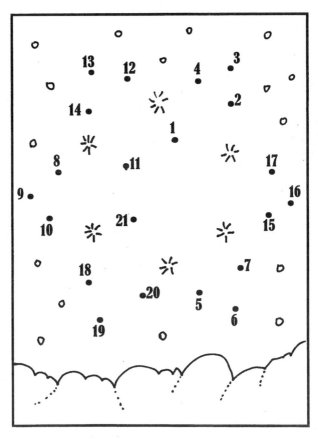

You may see one of these on Christmas. Careful,
it melts fast!

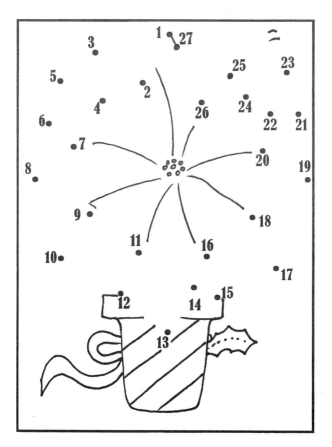

Many people like to buy this plant at Christmas time.
Follow the dots to see it.

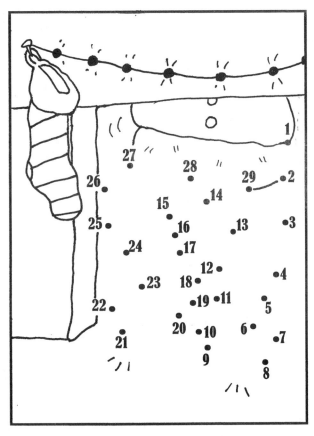

Who is that coming down the chimney? Draw a
picture by following the dots.

This elf is wearing something that belongs to Santa.
It is much too big!

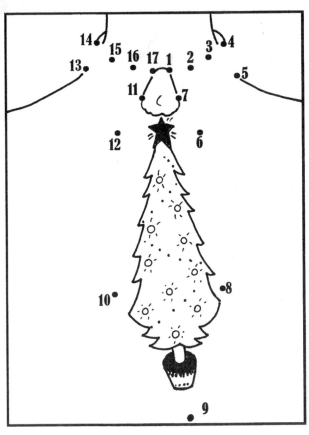

What is this man wearing to a special family
gathering? Follow the dots to find out.

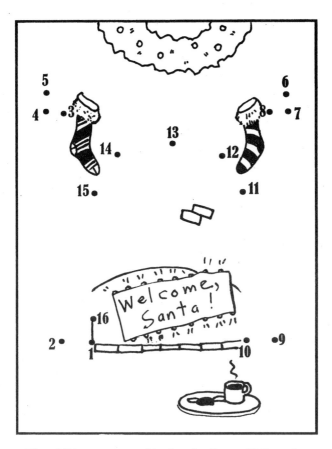

The children put out this sign for Santa. Follow the dots to see just where it is in the house.

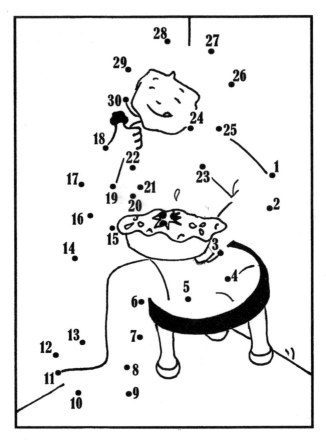

Who is enjoying a special Christmas treat? Connect the dots to find out.

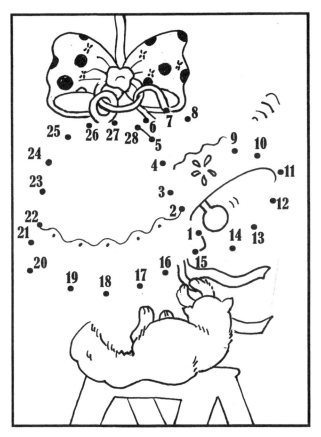

Kitty likes playing with these. They make such a nice sound! What are they?

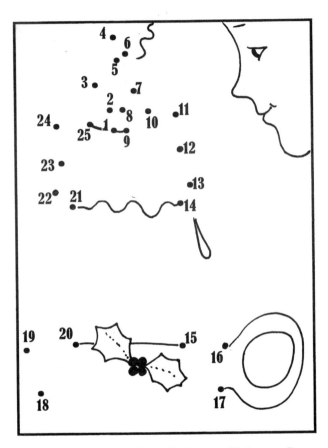

You might see this in a window on Christmas. It burns so brightly.

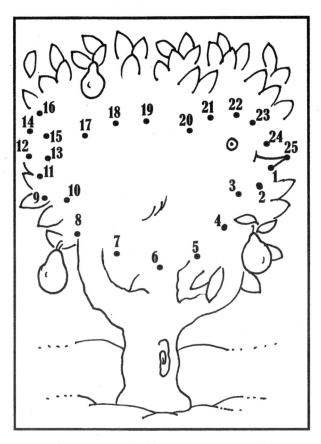

There's something in this pear tree. Do you know
what it is?

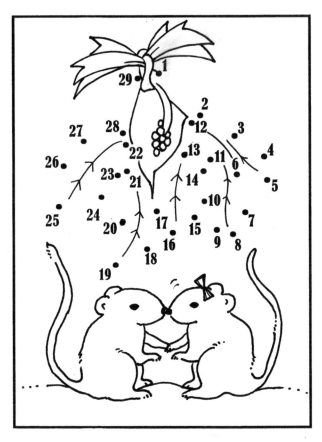

These little mice are standing under a special
Christmas plant. Follow the dots to see it.

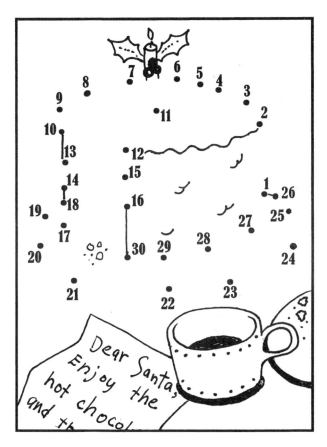

Connect the dots to see a picture of the yummy treat
the children left for Santa!

This elf is getting something ready for Santa. Follow the dots to see what it is.

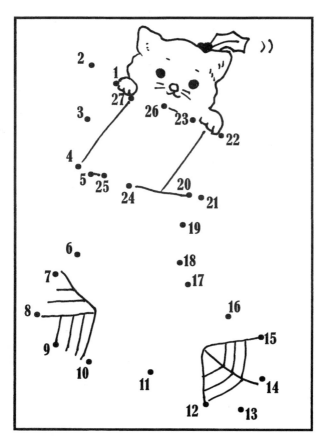

What is Kitty peeking out of? Follow the dots to find out.

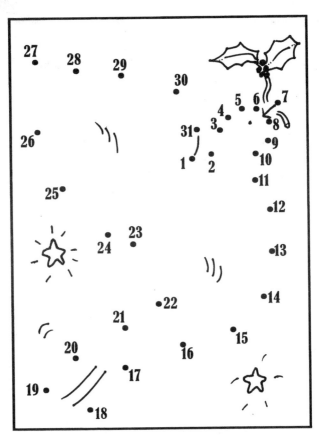

Many people think that this bird stands for peace.
What is it?

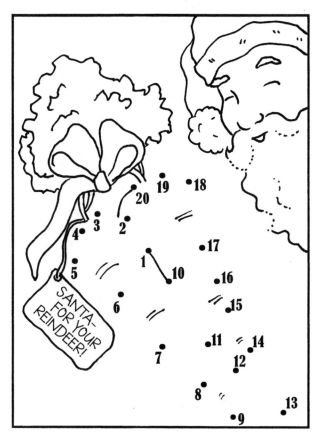

Here is a special treat for Santa's reindeer. Follow the
dots to see what it is.

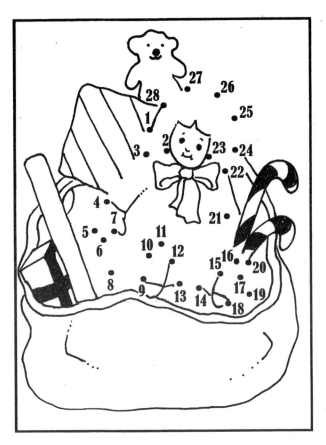

Follow the dots to see a present that a child will surely like.

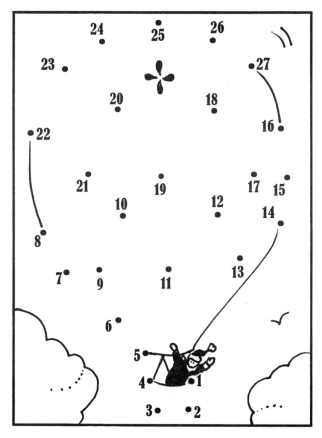

Here is another way that Santa can reach children in faraway places.

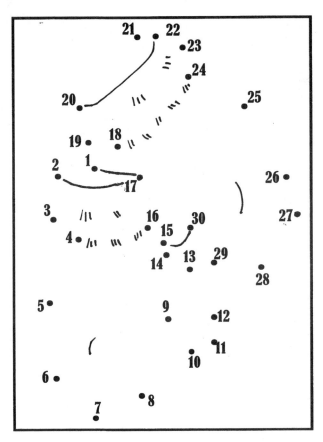

These will keep your hands warm during the winter.
Follow the dots to see a picture.

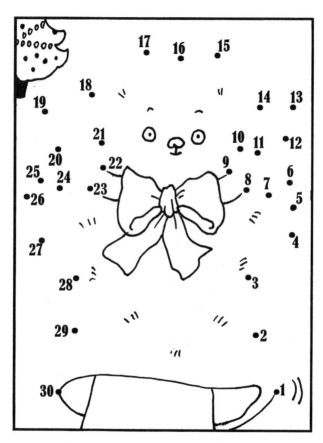

This toy fits over your hand. You can make it move.
What can it be?

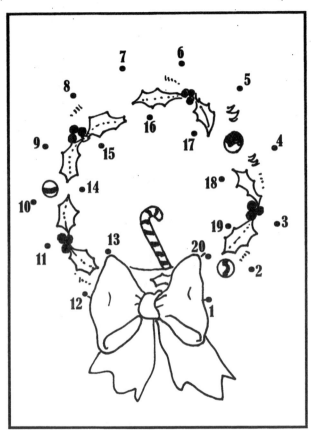

Some families hang this on their door at Christmas time. What is it?

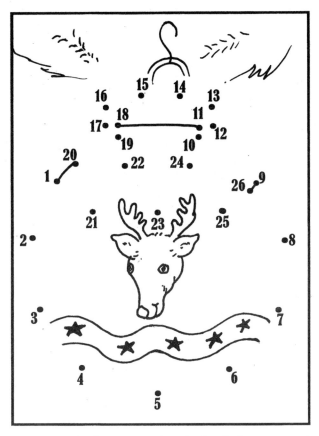

Connect the dots to see what the family has put on their Christmas tree.

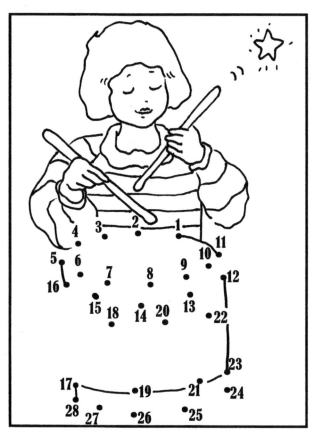

Kim loves this present that she got for Christmas.
What is it?

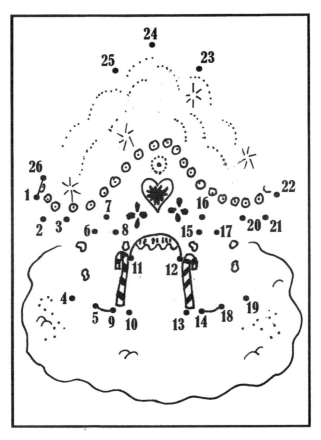

The children had so much fun making this treat.
Connect the dots to see a picture.

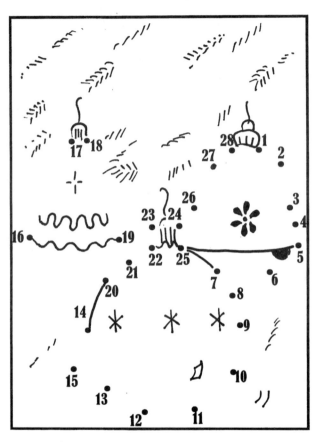

The children hung these on their Christmas tree last night. What are they?

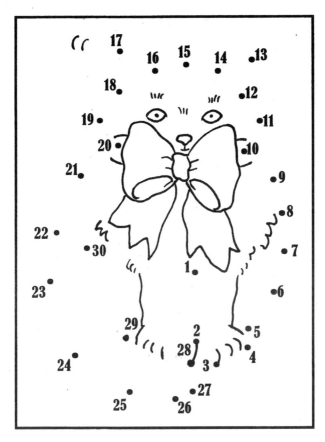

Follow the dots to see who gets dressed up for
Christmas.

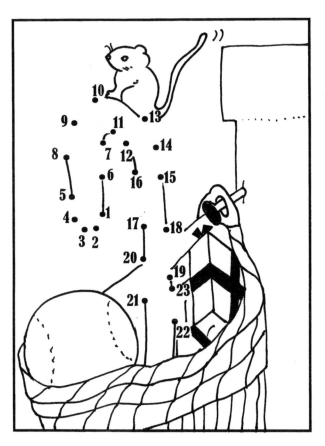

There is a sweet treat in each Christmas stocking.
Follow the dots to see what it is.

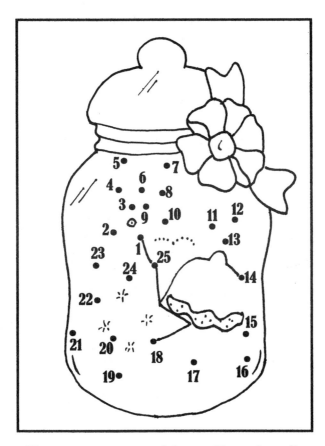

Here are some more special treats. To see them all,
follow the dots.

Connect the letters and dots and you will see who pulls Santa's sleigh on Christmas Eve!

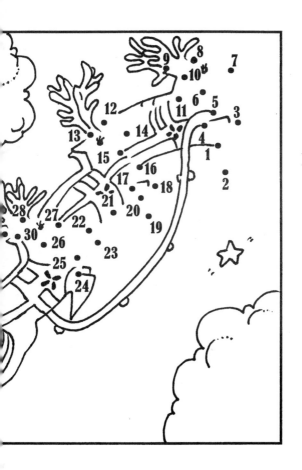

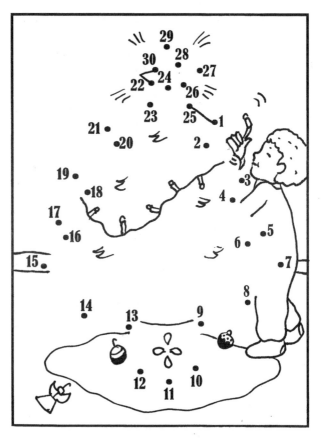

Nick is getting something ready for Christmas Day.
Follow the dots to see what it is.

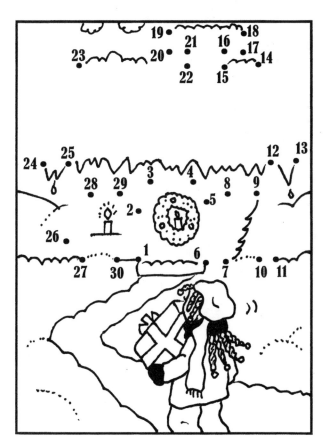

Carla can't wait to get to this place, where it is warm
and cozy. What is it?

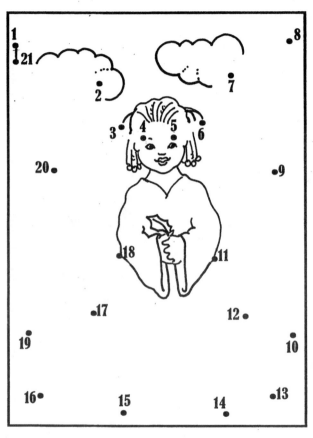

Follow the dots to complete this picture and see who is bringing good cheer at Christmas time.

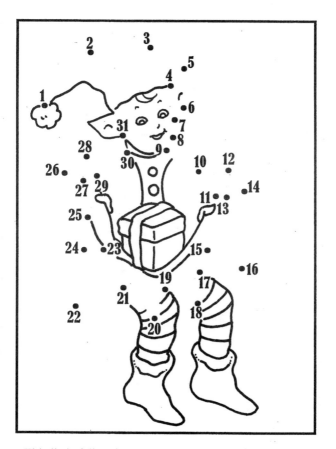

This little fellow has a present to put under the tree.
Connect the dots to see him.

Here is something that Santa can use to get home in a hurry. Merry Christmas!

Identifying the Pictures

When you follow the dots, these are what you will find.